Kinds of Unbelief

DUANE SHERIFF

Kinds *of* Unbelief

(and their cures)

COPYRIGHT

ISBN: 9798345242841
Printed in the United States of America
© 2024 by Victory Life Church
PO Box 427
Durant, OK 74702
dsm@pastorduane.com
580.634.5665

Contents

Introduction	1
Demon Possessed Son	4
Jairus	7
No Mixture	8
Unbelief #1 – The Rejection of Jesus	13
Unbelief #2 – Lack of Knowledge	20
Unbelief #3 – The Wrong Knowledge	27
Unbelief #4 – Carnality	37
Prayer and Fasting	45
Symptoms of Unbelief	49
Conclusion	53

Introduction

Jesus said to him, "If you can believe, all things are possible to him who believes."

Mark 9:23

The thought of all things being possible to me, if I can only believe, brings excitement and endless possibilities to my imagination. The potential of living a life of faith makes Christianity a true adventure into the promises and blessings of the Lord. Unfortunately, the early years in my Christian walk were centered around works and legalism versus grace and faith. The necessity of Hebrews 11:6 was never taught— *"But without faith it is **impossible** to please Him, for he who comes to God must believe that He is, and that He is a rewarder of those who diligently seek Him."* While all things are possible by faith, pleasing God is impossible without faith. The fact that there are rewards in seeking God was a foreign concept to me. I sincerely desired to please Him but didn't realize that my desire needed to be centered in faith, not performance or good works. I was taught that it was difficult to please God but if I tried hard and long enough, I could eventually earn His good pleasure. You can imagine my utter shock when I came across this scripture and realized it was IMPOSSIBLE to please Him without faith. Even if I had good works, it wasn't bringing pleasure to God without FAITH.

Faith is vital to our walk with God (2 Cor. 5:7). It is how we are justified in His sight (Hab. 2:4 / Rom. 1:17 / Gal 3:11 / Heb. 10:38). It is how we are saved (Eph. 2:8) and it is the substance of anything ever hoped for (Heb. 11:1). On many occasions Jesus taught regarding healing that, "Their faith made them whole" (Matt. 8:13 / 9:22 / 9:29 / 15:28). Faith is what makes the impossibilities we face in life possible with God (Mk 9:23). That truth is so exciting to us and our journey into God's promises and blessings.

So, if faith is vital to the life of the believer in Christ, what keeps the Church from living by faith in our daily lives? The enemy of our faith is unbelief. It has been said that fear is the opposite of faith, but fear is actually an emotional symptom of unbelief.

2 Kinds of Unbelief

Fear shows where we have trouble believing what God says. It is unbelief that hinders our faith, not necessarily too little faith. Jesus taught that even faith as small as a mustard seed was sufficient to see miracles happen, so Christians don't need more or bigger faith to see God move, but rather we need to eradicate unbelief from our thinking. We really don't have a faith problem but rather an unbelief problem. Every born-again believer has the very faith of Jesus in their spirit:

I am crucified with Christ; nevertheless I live; yet not I but Christ liveth in me: and the life which I now live in the flesh I live by **the faith** *of the Son of God, who loved me, and gave Himself for me. I do not frustrate the grace of God; for if righteousness come by the law then Christ is dead in vain.*

Galatians 2:20-21 KJV

The faith of Jesus is more than enough to move any mountain or bring into manifestation the promises of God. In Romans 12:3 (KJV) Paul declares— "God hath dealt to every man the measure of faith." The faith God gave us as a gift at the new birth is more than enough faith for any situation we face. We simply need to feed our faith and starve our unbelief. To do that we must discern different kinds of unbelief and their cures.

The following two stories from the life of Jesus will lay a foundation for understanding Jesus' work as it relates to faith and unbelief. After examining these Gospel accounts, we will identify four types of unbelief and the cures for them.

Demon Possessed Son

Mark 9:17 (KJV) is where we find the story of a man with a demon possessed son— *"And one of the multitude answered and said, Master, I have brought unto thee my son, which hath a dumb spirit."* This boy is deaf and cannot speak because of demonic influence. His father explains to Jesus that when this spirit manifests it seizes him causing him to foam at the mouth, gnash his teeth, and become rigid. The father had brought the boy to the disciples to be healed but to no avail. In seeming frustration, Jesus looks at the disciples and in Mark 9:19 (KJV) responds, *"O faithless generation, how long shall I be with you? How long shall I suffer you? Bring him unto Me."* At times, like in this verse, Jesus deals firmly with His followers. He doesn't look at His disciples and say, "Hey, no problem boys. This is a mega major demon. It's over your pay grade so don't worry about it; I'll take care of it." No, He calls them a faithless generation and expects them to learn from this moment. He reminds them that He won't always be physically present with them to intervene. He will be with them in spirit and empower them by the Holy Spirit, but He knows they will have to deal with demons. They will have to deal with bringing the kingdom of God into the kingdom of this world, so they had better learn from his example while He walks with them. He rebukes and corrects them. Jesus then turns His attention back to the father and his son:

> *Then they brought him to Him. And when he saw Him, immediately the spirit convulsed him, and he fell on the ground and wallowed, foaming at the mouth. So He asked his father, "How long has this been happening to him?" And he said, "From childhood. And often he has*

thrown him both into the fire and into the water to destroy him. But if You can do anything, have compassion on us and help us." Jesus said to him, "If you can believe, all things are possible to him who believes." Immediately the father of the child cried out and said with tears, **"Lord, I believe; help my unbelief."**

Mark 9:20-24

Jesus then rebuked the evil spirit, and it came out of the boy.

God's willingness to save us, heal us, and prosper us is never at question. God's ability to absolutely transform our lives is never the issue. Our ability to "believe" is what comes into question. The good news is that we can learn to believe only and allow God's power and ability to flow into our lives. So God isn't the problem here, we are. That is not to condemn us or make us feel bad; remember— *"There is therefore now no condemnation to those who are in Christ Jesus, who do not walk according to the flesh but according to the Spirit"* (Rom. 8:1). Many times, Jesus was blunt and could sound hard or condemning but His desire is to help us and deal with our inaccurate thought processes. When He looked at the disciples and called them a faithless generation, He followed that remark with the encouragement that all things are possible to those who believe. So, the next time obstacles or circumstances come our way that seem impossible we need to remember this admonishment and trust God. We need to learn how to be established in our faith then know that we are going to see the things of God come to pass in our lives. The father of this child cried out to Jesus and told Him, "I believe, help my unbelief." We've all been there, right? When we are trusting God, but doubt is creeping in canceling out our belief, we can ask God to help us with our unbelief and move to the mindset of "believe only."

Jairus

Luke 8 tells another story that helps us understand the role of faith. Jairus was a ruler of the synagogue whose only daughter at twelve years old was sick and dying. Jairus seeks out Jesus, falls down at His feet, and begs Him to come to his house and heal her. While Jairus seeks the Lord's help, word comes to not bother the Master because his daughter has died. Luke 8:50 tells us, *"But when Jesus heard it, He answered him, saying, 'Do not be afraid;* **only believe***, and she will be made well.'"* Jesus was encouraging him to believe only. Jairus did and his daughter was made whole! The admonition to "believe only" implies you can believe and not believe at the same time, a blend which hinders believing. We need to believe **only** and not doubt in our hearts in order to see God's power in our lives (Mk. 11:23).

No Mixture

In my journey of learning how to deal with unbelief, I discovered different kinds of unbelief that are in the Bible and their cures. I knew I didn't want to "fake it till I make it," nor keep confessing something trying to make it happen on my own strength or merit. For example, if I felt like I had done enough good works to earn a new Cadillac and I started confessing, "Cadillac come, Cadillac come" thinking my confession would make it happen, that would not be faith. I understood that kind of believing was a form of legalism, and I didn't want any part of it. I wanted to be honest with God and myself when I struggled and receive His instruction in building my faith. Some people believe that their confession alone can make things happen or change. However, it is faith in God's power and promises that changes things. While faith speaks, speaking is not always faith. Paul tells us in 2 Corinthians 4:13, *"And since we have the same spirit of faith, according to what is written, 'I Believed and therefore I spoke,' we also believe and therefore speak."* We believe first then our faith speaks, changing things in our lives. But believing and unbelieving cancel one another out. They do not mix.

Under the Old Testament law, people were not allowed to plow their fields with an ox and a donkey yoked together (Deut. 22:10). Clean and unclean could not be mixed. People were forbidden to sow their fields with mixed seed (Deut. 22:9). People were not to wear garments of different fabrics, such as wool and linen together (Deut. 22:11). The priests could only wear linen because they could not sweat when ministering to the Lord. Wool would create sweat and that was unacceptable to the Lord. The two could not mix. As Christians who did not grow up under Old Testament laws, we sometimes lose valuable insights into how God works in relationship with His covenant people. Even seemingly obscure laws can foreshadow the work that Jesus would accomplish under the New Covenant. Linen, the fabric of the priests, was a type of faith in God's grace (no sweat on our part). Wool was a type of unbelief or legalism (us working and sweating to receive from God). If a person tried to mix clean and unclean items under the old covenant, the entire lot was defiled. Likewise, when we try to mix belief and unbelief, we defile our spiritual harvest (Deut. 22:9). These Old Testament examples were types and shadows pointing to Jesus and our trust in Him.

The concept of no mixture continues in the New Testament. Paul taught the early Church about not being unequally yoked to unbelievers, Satan, or any form of darkness (2 Cor. 6:14-16). Faith and doubt do not mix and believing and unbelieving cancel each other out. We must believe only to see God's blessings and power work in our lives. Jesus taught that the light of our body must be single, or pure, to experience God's fullness— *"The lamp of the body is the eye. If therefore your eye is good, your whole body will be full of light. But if your eye is bad, your whole body will be full of darkness. If therefore the light that is in you is darkness, how great is that darkness!"* (Matt. 6:22-23).

In the summer of 2018, I had to practice this kind of pure faith in a radical way. Our family faced a seemingly impossible situation that tried our faith and sent us continually to the throne to obtain grace to help in our time of need (Heb. 4:16). Our grandson, Urias, died during childbirth and remained dead for twenty minutes after birth. He was raised from the dead after a total of thirty minutes; however, all his organs were damaged, and he was having critical seizures. While everyone was touched deeply by his coming back to life miracle, the doctors were offering little hope for his recovery. All his organs were critically damaged and not functioning properly. It was a spiritual battle that our whole family engaged in fighting for his life. All of us had to stand against doubt and believe only for a miracle and restoration of his entire being. We fought and stood as a family and with our church family that joined in this fight. In twenty-one days, we were able to take Urias home, a healed boy that continues to remind us of God's grace to help in our time of need. His life is a testimony that all things are possible to those who believe. HALLELUJAH!!

I desire to see each believer learn how to have a pure faith, unmixed with unbelief and doubt. We all can tell stories of God's miraculous power when we learn to believe only. Now, let's begin to deal with these four kinds of unbelief and discover their cures. There has been much confusion concerning unbelief and how to deal with it, so I desire to help clear up any misunderstandings that can keep us from believing only. We will dive into how to aggressively attack these enemies of our faith and stand firm.

Unbelief #1
The Rejection of Jesus

The first kind of unbelief is found in John 16:7-11—
*"Nevertheless I tell you the truth. It is **to your advantage** that I go away; for if I do not go away, the Helper will not come to you; but if I depart, I will send Him to you. And when He has come, He will convict the world of sin, and of righteousness, and of judgment: of sin, because **they do not believe in Me**; of righteousness, because I go to My Father and you see Me no more; of judgment, because the ruler of this world is judged."* Wow! Can you imagine standing there with the disciples and being told that Jesus was going away, and it would be better for them that way? How could that be true? Didn't He hold the words of life? There were miracles everywhere He went; how could it be preferred that He be gone?

Jesus was trying to explain to them that He had to fulfill His mission on earth through His death, burial, and resurrection. In doing this, He would go to the Father and send the Holy Spirit to be with them and in them never to go away again (Jn. 14:16).

Jesus knew it would be better, because He would live His life in a body of believers worldwide, never again limited to one geographical location. These believers would do the works of Jesus and greater works (Jn. 14:12). That same Spirit would convict the world of sin. Notice that Jesus said the Spirit would bring conviction of "sin" (singular), not "sins" (plural). What is the sin He convicts them of? Not believing in Him. The only sin not covered on the cross is the rejection of the cross itself: not believing that Jesus came, lived a perfect life, died on the cross and shed His blood as an atonement for sin, being resurrected and now seated in Heaven. Religion tries to deal with individual sins, such as smoking, claiming it will send you to hell. Folks, smoking will not send you to hell. It may make you smell like you have been there, but it will not send you to a devil's hell. I'm not saying smoking or drinking or doing drugs is okay. Quitting those things is good, but will not get you to heaven nor send you to hell. It is not our sins that condemn us to hell, it is unbelief! It's not our good works that gets us to heaven, it's our belief! Believing in Jesus and Him dying for our sins saves us and unbelief in

Him condemns us. The only sin sending people to hell is the rejection of what Jesus did at the cross. This is what the Holy Spirit was sent for, to convict us of the sin of unbelief (rejecting Jesus and the cross).

In Mark 16:15-16 Jesus tells His disciples, *"Go into all the world and preach the gospel to every creature. He who* **believes** *and is baptized will be saved; but he who does* **not believe** *will be condemned."* This further illustrates that unbelief in Jesus and His work on the cross (where all of our sins were paid for) is the sin that condemns people to a devil's hell. Again, in John 3:18 Jesus says, *"He who* **believes** *in Him is not condemned; but he who* **does not believe** *is condemned already, because he has* **not believed** *in the name of the only begotten Son of God."* This is another confirmation and witness that the rejection of Jesus as God's sacrifice for all sins is what sentences someone to eternal damnation. Jesus deals with this sin and calls it an unforgivable sin in Mark 3:28-29— *"Assuredly, I say to you,* **all sins** *will be forgiven the sons of men, and whatever blasphemies they may utter; but he who blasphemes against the Holy Spirit* **never has forgiveness**, *but is* *subject to eternal condemnation."* The only sin the Holy Spirit convicts the world of is the rejection of Jesus and the cross (unbelief). If someone blasphemes Him and commits this sin of unbelief, then the sacrifice made for all their other sins avails nothing. Rejecting Jesus in unbelief is rejecting what He did to atone for all our sins. Either Jesus dies and pays for all our sins, or we will pay for all our sins. In His holiness God must judge all sins or He denies His own nature. His justice meets His mercy at the cross in Jesus dying for our sins. If one rejects that payment in Jesus, then they face the debt of sin before God.

Luke 12:8-10 deals with this sin as well. In verses eight and nine Jesus speaks of our open and public confession of Him before men. Then He declares how He will acknowledge us before the angels of God. He goes on to say in verse ten, *"And anyone who speaks a word against the Son of Man, it will be forgiven him; but to him who blasphemes against the Holy Spirit,* **it will not be forgiven.***"* So, what is blasphemy of the Holy Ghost? It is the rejection of the cross and unbelief in who Jesus is and what He did. Any and all sins can be forgiven in Christ, but this sin of unbelief cannot be forgiven. It is the Holy Spirit that convicts of this sin and to reject that conviction is to blaspheme the Holy Spirit. This is often referred to as the "unpardonable sin."

I can't tell you how many people have come to me in tears fearing they had committed an "unpardonable sin," not understanding what that really is. If you think you've committed this sin, you haven't. Those who commit it, know it. You can't accidentally reject Jesus. This sin is the willful rejection of the Holy Spirit's conviction of who Jesus is. So once more, let me be very clear. The only unpardonable or unforgivable sin is the rejection of Jesus and the cross where all sins were paid for. Blaspheme of the Holy Spirit is refusing to accept God's love for you, the atonement, and Jesus as Lord of your life. There are not many ways to forgiveness of sins or to heaven. There is only one way and that is Jesus as is made clear in John 14:6— *"Jesus said to him, 'I am the way, the truth, and the life. No one comes to the Father except through Me."* People think this is being dogmatic or narrow-minded, but the

Word is very clear. There is only one person that was God made flesh that could die for our sins and be raised from the dead for our justification. God says, "Look, I've paid for all your sins through my blood sacrifice and given you the gift of eternal life. Now the choice is yours; if you believe you will be saved, if you don't believe you will be damned." As Acts 4:12 states, *"Nor is there salvation in any other, for there is no other name under heaven given among men by which we must be saved."*

THE CURE

The gospel and preaching the cross is the cure for the unbelief of rejecting Jesus. Paul knew the power of the gospel and Christ's redemptive work. He declares, *"For I am not ashamed of the gospel of Christ, for it is the power of God to salvation for everyone who believes, for the Jew first and also for the Greek"* (Romans 1:16). Paul also taught, *"For the message of the cross is foolishness to those who are perishing, but to us who are being saved it is the power of God."* (1 Corinthians 1:18).

The only cure is faith in Jesus and His complete work of the cross for all our sins. Answering the crowd on the day of Pentecost on what they must do to be saved, Peter said— *"Repent and let everyone of you be baptized in the name of Jesus Christ for the remission of sins and you shall receive the gift of the Holy Spirit"* (Acts 2:38). Later, in Acts 3:19, Peter urged his fellow Israelites to *"Repent therefore and be converted that your sins may be blotted out."* When we repent of our sins and call upon the name of Jesus, all our sins are washed away, to be remembered no more. Hallelujah!

This is the cure as verified in Romans 10:9-10— *"if you confess with your mouth the Lord Jesus and believe in your heart that God has raised Him from the dead, you will be saved. For with the heart one believes unto righteousness, and with the mouth confession is made unto salvation."* It truly is that simple.

This is not the unbelief the father with the demon possessed son demonstrated. If it had been, he wouldn't have come to the disciples in the first place and then persisted in bringing his son to Jesus. He believed Jesus was the Messiah and could heal but he was honest in saying that there was some unbelief he was battling.

Unbelief #2
Lack of Knowledge

The second kind of unbelief is the easiest for me to deal with in ministry. It is one I've had to deal with my whole life. This type of unbelief is having a lack of knowledge. In Hosea 4:6 God says, *"My people are destroyed for lack of knowledge."* We cannot believe for anything independent of knowing God's will for our lives. His Word is His will and gives us the knowledge we need in order to believe.

What we don't know can be a huge hindrance to our faith. For example, Paul meets some disciples of John and asks them in Acts 19:2, *"'Did you receive the Holy Spirit when you believed?' So they said to him, 'We have not so much as heard whether there is a Holy Spirit.'"* Unfortunately, there are entire churches that can make that same confession. You cannot believe to receive the Holy Spirit if you haven't heard God's Word concerning receiving Him. Healing is the same way. If you don't know God's will regarding healing, how can you believe God for it? What you don't know CAN hurt you. For years as a Christian, I didn't know it was God's will to heal. Because I didn't have a knowledge of this I never asked for healing or believed for it, so I never received healing in my body. Then I heard God's Word concerning His will to heal and faith came with this knowledge. I began to experience healing in my body as well as praying for healing for other people's bodies. The same is true of prosperity and God's will to prosper us in this life. I was perishing in poverty because I didn't have a knowledge of God's will to prosper me. Once I heard His will to prosper me, I believed and began to experience success in my life. God brought success in ministry, my family, my friendships, and on and on I could go. This is the kind of unbelief I enjoy helping people with the most as a pastor. I can't tell you the joy I experience when I see lights come on in individuals when they realize the truth of God's Word and all that He has for them in this life. I see faith rising in their hearts and them beginning to walk in the blessings of God.

Forgiveness of sin is like that. Until we know God's Word on how complete and perfect the sacrifice of Jesus was for our sins, we struggle with unbelief that we are truly forgiven. How do we overcome falling, failing, making mistakes, and thinking that God may be holding our sin against us? When we look at Scripture and understand the full atonement of Jesus Christ then we realize that we have been forgiven of past, present, and future tense sins. Now if we make mistakes, we can run boldly to the throne of grace to obtain mercy and help in time of need. There is no greater time of need than when we mess up. But if we don't hear of God's great mercy and help from the Word, then we won't have faith to overcome in our time of need. So few Christians seem to know how forgiven, blessed, and accepted by God they really are. Many Christians don't have a knowledge of God's love for them and how God is for them and never against them. Their unbelief isn't deliberate, but rather a product of not knowing better. We must understand that God is not angry with us but loves us with an unconditional love. We have been made righteous and truly holy in the eyes of God. Paul instructs believers to, *"Awake to righteousness and do not sin; for some do not have the knowledge of God. I speak this to your shame"* (1 Cor. 15:34). We only overcome sin and live holy lives when we see the righteousness of God we have already been made in Christ (2 Cor. 5:21 / Rom. 5:19). It is such a shame so many good believers do not have this knowledge and struggle unnecessarily with guilt and condemnation. In our culture today people are perishing, and many have not heard the truth so faith can come for them to be saved, healed, delivered, or prosperous.

THE CURE

The good news is that there is a cure for this kind of unbelief, and it is found in Romans 10:17: *"So then faith comes by hearing, and hearing by the word of God."* Your faith begins and ends where the Word of God is known. A knowledge of God's love and complete forgiveness will cure this kind of unbelief. Let's look at John 8:31-32, *"Then Jesus said to those Jews who believed Him, 'If you abide in My word, you are My disciples indeed. And you shall* **know the truth***, and the truth shall make you free.'"* Knowing the truth will set us free from doubt and unbelief and enable us to believe for good things in our lives. As mentioned here in 2 Peter 1:2-3— *"Grace and peace be multiplied to you in the* *knowledge of God* *and of Jesus our Lord, as His divine* *power has given to us all things that pertain to life and* *godliness,* **through the knowledge of Him** *who called* *us by glory and virtue."* This fact that God's power has given us everything we need to live a godly life can only be enjoyed by knowing this truth and receiving it by faith.

My first experience as a pastor was in the Methodist church and I had this false perception that the congregation had rejected the truth of God's Word. Dumb, right? I have repented of this false impression because when I started ministering on the Holy Spirit, healing, and God's love for us, they were on the edge of their seats. I realized that they hadn't rejected these truths—they had never heard them. I began to teach on God's love, His will to heal, prosper, and deliver us. I taught them how to fight the good fight of faith, walking by faith and not by sight. The truths concerning the armor of God and standing amidst affliction and hardship were brand new concepts to them. The church began to grow as people were hungry to hear the truth and gain knowledge so they could walk in freedom.

The great lesson I learned from this was that I can never assume people have rejected God's Word or truth ever again; I simply must be obedient to share truth and let the choice be theirs to receive or reject it. In fear of being rejected ourselves, we cannot reject the truth for others. They have a right to hear the truth spoken to them in love then choose to receive it or reject it. We have to ask ourselves the same questions that Paul asks in Romans 10:14, *"How then shall they call on Him in whom they have not believed? And how shall they believe in Him of whom* **they have not heard?** *And how shall they hear without a preacher?"* The preacher must share the truth of God's Word in love for them to believe. Many are suffering in unbelief because they have not heard God's Word so faith can come. As we know, *"faith comes by hearing, and hearing by the word of God"* (Rom. 10:17).

Again, the cure for this kind of unbelief is the teaching of God's Word and speaking the truth in love (Eph. 4:15). Jesus actually experienced this kind of unbelief in His own hometown. In Mark 6:4 He says, *"A prophet is not without honor except in his own country, among his own relatives, and in his own house."* We have a cultural phrase that encompasses Jesus' meaning here: "familiarity breeds contempt." When Jesus went to Nazareth and taught in the synagogue He was rejected because they saw Him as "the carpenter," a son of Mary. The fact that they knew and lived among His family made them miss the significance of God's Kingdom at hand. Mark goes on to say in verses five and six, *"Now He could do no mighty work there, except that He laid His hands on a few sick people and healed them. And He marveled because of **their unbelief.**"* The Scriptures only record two instances where Jesus marveled. Once, Jesus marveled at great faith He saw in a Roman Centurion (Matt. 8:10), but in this account, He marvels at such great unbelief. What was His solution? Mark 6:6b tells us, *"Then He went about the villages in a circuit, teaching."* Teaching the Word of God (truth) causes faith to arise in the human heart, setting us free from doubt and unbelief. I pray Jesus is marveling at our great faith, and not our unbelief.

Unbelief #3
The Wrong Knowledge
(Lies & Deception)

The only thing worse than a lacking knowledge is believing the wrong knowledge. The third kind of unbelief is having the wrong knowledge, and in my experience, it is the most difficult to overcome. Most people in this state of unbelief are usually contentious, confrontational, and want to debate. They are convinced that the lies they believe are actually the truth. They will resist God's mercy and goodness, insisting that God is the one making them sick, poor, and putting trials, tribulations, and hardships on them. They believe that God is doing bad things to them to teach them something. Their image of God is more like the retributive "Godfather" versus the loving Father God. This belief system is rooted in lies and deceptions and tends to become a stronghold in individuals and sometimes entire churches. What is a stronghold? Anything that has a strong hold on a person.

Strongholds are opinions and philosophies of men that are contrary to God's Word and nature. Strongholds get built when we are living in this type of unbelief.

These strongholds must be pulled down. 2 Corinthians 10:4 says, *"For the weapons of our warfare are not carnal but mighty in God for **pulling down strongholds**."* Some people believe that strongholds are demons. Strongholds are not demons; however, demons can traffic within them. The Scriptures teach that strongholds must be pulled down and that demons must be cast out. They are both enemies of the light, but demons and strongholds are not the same thing.

The ancient Hebrews defined a stronghold as a castle or fort (Strongs #4679 – *metsad*). In the Greek language a stronghold was a means to fortify through the idea of holding safely (Strongs #3794 – *okhooromah*). Like the Hebrew definition, it could refer to a castle or a military fortress. In the fleeing of Saul, David was said to have dwelt in strongholds (1 Sam. 23:14 / 19 / 29). So David hid from a physical enemy in a physical stronghold, but in the

New Testament, Paul applies the idea of a stronghold to our thinking. While God's Kingdom advances, strongholds are arguments and philosophies that Satan hides behind. They are mental castles or fortified cities of unbelief in our hearts (2 Sam. 24:7).

People with this form of unbelief hold fast to the traditions of men that make the Word of God of no effect in their lives (Mark 7:13). They look you in the eye and say things like, "I don't care what the Bible says, this is what I believe. I don't care what the Scriptures say, this is how I feel, or this has been my experience." Or they'll say, "This is what my church believes and how I was taught." Some of you may think people like this don't exist, but I am telling you they do, and there are even entire churches stuck in this kind of unbelief.

One time I was trying to help a fellow pastor with some cultural issues. He struggled with what I was telling him from the Word and said to me, "look, you can make the Bible say anything you want it to say." While there may be some legitimacy to that logic or argument, it is also true that God has said certain things that are absolute truth and will never change, no matter how hard some may try to change it.

In Mark 7:7 Jesus was basically telling the Pharisees and scribes that their worship of Him was a farce, and they had taken the precepts of man and made them doctrines of God. Mark 7:13 tells us that these manmade traditions essentially nullified the Word of God in their lives. When we exalt ideas from our culture or traditions, they become strongholds that cancel out God's Word and work.

Today, many people have believed lies about God and themselves for so long that it is hard to let go. I understand this struggle. When I met my wife, Sue, and turned my life back to God, He supernaturally delivered me from my strongholds. However, there were some lingering deceptions such as a poverty mindset that I had to pull down with the Lord's help. There were also lies about myself that I had believed for so long, and it took time to break those off my life. I struggled to believe that God could—and wanted to—use me for His Kingdom, because I had been bound by the lie that

I was unworthy, damaged goods. I was deceived and this belief about myself was actually unbelief and had to be reversed. There were other lies I believed, like I could never overcome certain issues because it was just how my family was and always had been. Even when someone would try to tell me how precious I was to God, the strongholds and demonic trafficking in those strongholds kept me bound. It took time, but through God's grace and Word I was able to pull those down and believe what the Bible says about me. Many people experience these same things and go through sin cycles. They get victory over sin and walk free for a week or two then fall right back into it. This form of unbelief hinders so many Christians because tearing down strongholds is not often an easy or quick work. It requires diligence to pull those strongholds down.

THE CURE

So, how do you cure these traditions of men that have made the Word of God of no effect? How do you cure people that have believed and continue to believe a lie? To believe a lie about God, the devil, or ourselves is unbelief. This form of unbelief will never be pulled down until one gets a passion for and commitment to the truth. In simplicity, this is how I pulled these strongholds down in my life. Only a love for the truth will break the power of those lies. Jesus declares in John 8:44 that Satan is a liar and the father of all lies and says, *"he does not stand in the truth, because there is no truth in him."* The enemy cannot abide in the truth, so it is the truth and knowing it that sets us free from this unbelief.

In 2 Thessalonians 2:10, we see how people were being deceived and perished—*"because they did not receive the **love** of the truth, that they might be saved."* Verse twelve goes on to say, *"that they may be condemned who did not believe the **truth**, but had pleasure in unrighteousness."* It is love for the truth that delivers us from unbelief because all unbelief is rooted in a lie. Being humble and submitting to the truth delivers us.

2 Corinthians 10:4-5 explains the process and building of a stronghold, which also helps us understand how to dismantle one: *"For the weapons of our warfare are not carnal, but mighty through God to the*

pulling down of strong holds; casting down imaginations, and every high thing that exalteth itself against the knowledge of God, and bringing into captivity every thought to the obedience of Christ."

The Process of a Stronghold:

Thought-----------------------------------Secular versus Biblical

High Thing----------------------------------What do you exalt?

Imagination----------------------You see it in your soul (images)

Stronghold------------A place of refuge from an ensuing enemy

Is what you believe a lie or truth? Are you going to exalt it above God's Word or repent (change your mind)? Are you going to meditate on the truth or the lie? Are you going to yield to the truth and allow Holy Spirit to renew your mind? It is essential to displace old, exalted thoughts and replace them with new thoughts based on the truth of God's Word.

One time I shared a message that offended a man and afterward told me, "I've been thinking this way longer than you've been alive." Number one, that was a long time to be wrong. Number two, thinking wrong for a long time won't make it right. It is a lot like preaching; longer won't make it better! If it's bad, cut it short. We have to be willing to surrender our thoughts to God, even if they have been with us for a lifetime.

Romans 3:3-4 helps us understand how to cure the strongholds of unbelief that hold us: *"For what if some did not believe? Shall their unbelief make the faith of God without effect? God forbid: yea,* **let God be true,** *but every man a liar."* The Word of God must be exalted above man's word—above our thoughts, feelings, or circumstances. God's Word must become absolute authority and truth in our lives in order to overcome these strongholds in our hearts and in society.

The truth may be costly in these days of lies, deception, fraud, fake news, corrupt politicians, and unethical professors. Jesus was clear concerning the cost of discipleship in Matthew 16:24-25— *"If anyone desires to come after Me, let him deny himself, and take up his cross, and follow Me. For whoever desires to save his life will lose it, but whoever loses his life for My sake will find it."* On another occasion Jesus spoke of bringing a sword instead of peace. In Matthew 10:34-38, Jesus says, *"Do not think that I came to bring peace on earth. I did not come to bring peace but a sword. For I have come to set a man against his father, a daughter against her mother, and a daughter-in-law against her mother-in-law; and a man's enemies will be those of his own household. He who loves father or mother* **more than Me** *is not worthy of Me. And he who loves son or daughter* **more than Me** *is not worthy of Me. And he who does not take his cross and follow after Me is not worthy of Me."* Today Satan is defiling the faith of an entire generation. Parents are having to choose who they love more, their children going WOKE or Jesus who has called us to be AWAKE.

God is dividing truth from lies. He has come to bring a sword and will set at odds anyone on opposing sides of His Word. Even within our families, a choice has to be made to love Jesus more than anyone else, even ourselves. This doesn't mean we don't love our spouse, our kids, or our community; it just means we have to love Jesus more. It means we must not deny Jesus and TRUTH even if it means making a stand that crosses a family member or those in our community. People today are bound by strongholds and demonic activity to the point they love them and resist pulling them down. The only reason truth makes us uncomfortable is because we have become comfortable with a lie. Even when it is countercultural, we must be willing to love the truth and submit each of our thoughts to God's Word. That is how we break the stronghold of unbelief.

Unbelief #4
Carnality
(Five Senses Driven)

The last kind of unbelief is carnality, a worldly mindset that is driven by the five senses. Let's look back at the story of the father with the demoniac son. Why did Jesus expect the disciples to cast that demon out? He didn't defend them or make excuses for them. Remember He didn't say to them, "It's okay boys, you weren't equipped for this; this is like a major mega demon and above your paygrade." No, He called them a faithless generation (Mk. 9:19). He had been preparing them to carry on the work of the Kingdom after He was gone and knew they had cast out demons in the past. In Luke 9:1, Jesus called His disciples together and gave them power and authority over **all** demons and to cure diseases. They had unlimited authority and power over all demons—not most but all! There were no demons they could not deal with according to Jesus' order: *"And as you go, preach, saying 'The kingdom of* *heaven is at hand.' Heal the sick, cleanse the lepers, raise the dead, cast out demons. Freely you have received, freely give"* (Matt. 10:7-8). The disciples had authority over all demons and had been casting them out before this man brought his son to them. They had been having success, but something changed. Jesus sent out seventy with certain instructions: *"And heal the sick there, and say to them, 'The kingdom of God has come near to you'"* (Luke 10:9). When they returned, they were full of joy and told the Lord that even the demons were subject to them in Jesus' name (Luke 10:17). This was not their first rodeo, so what changed? They had faith; however, when they went to cast this demon out the boy fell to the ground and started foaming at the mouth, gnashing his teeth and going into a seizure. Their senses (what they saw) overrode their faith. They were moved by what they saw rather than what they believed.

This is the kind of unbelief that most people struggle with; their carnal, unrenewed minds are subject to the flesh and five physical senses. We all know Christians who respond to what the Bible says with, "Yeah, I know, but this is how I feel." That is being dominated by senses rather than what God says.

The disciple Thomas also illustrates this kind of unbelief at work. After his fellow disciples claimed they had seen the Lord, Thomas boldly declares— *"Unless I **see** in His hands the print of the nails, and put my finger into the print of the nails, and put my hand into His side, I will not believe"* (Jn. 20:25). Notice how Thomas needed to **feel** something before he would believe. This kind of unbelief demands proof by senses and human reasoning (carnal mind) in order to confirm what is true. This kind of unbelief promotes human feelings and carnal understanding above all else. The carnal mind and five physical senses will not allow a person to walk on water—yet Peter did. Thomas was saying that unless he saw something and felt something in the natural world, he would not believe. After revealing Himself to Thomas, Jesus said, *"Thomas, because you have seen Me, you have believed. Blessed are those who have not seen and yet have believed"* (Jn. 20:29). This carnal way of thinking runs contrary to the Kingdom of God. As believers, we believe in a lot of things we cannot see such as heaven, angels, the cross, the resurrection, and even God Himself (1 Pet. 1:8).

The Apostle Paul instructs the church about the dangers of carnal thinking when he writes:

> *For those who live according to the flesh set their minds on the things of the flesh but those who live according to the Spirit, the things of the Spirit. For to be* **carnally minded is death***, but to be spiritually minded is life and peace. Because the carnal mind is* **enmity** *against God; for it is not subject to the law of God, nor indeed can be. So then, those who are in the flesh cannot please God.*

Romans 8:5-8

As born-again believers, we have the Spirit of Christ living on the inside of us. We can choose to walk after the Spirit. However, if we let our mind be ruled by carnal thinking then we walk after the flesh and the result is death. These Scriptures are not talking about dying naturally, which one day all of us will do if the Lord tarries. Death, as referred to here, is the consequences incurred due to unbelief. Death is a life given over to carnality and darkness.

We also need to understand that our carnal unrenewed minds will oppose God's Word, thus perpetuating this form of unbelief. Romans 8:6 again says, "to be carnally minded is death." And 1 Corinthians 2:14 says, *"But the natural man does not receive the things of the Spirit of God, for they are foolishness to him; nor can he know them, because they are spiritually discerned."* Our natural man will oppose the things of our spirit man.

This kind of unbelief prevails in our world today. We have exalted "feelings" to the point that identity confusion runs rampant. "I feel like girl today, so I must be one." Think of how ungodly that is yet it is all around us. What does that say to God? It is literally like shaking your fist in His face and saying, "I know you created me a boy in my mother's womb, but I believe I'm a girl because I feel like one." I'm not condemning anyone struggling with gender dysmorphia or their carnal feelings; but when did feelings become a god? How can we worship feelings and reject the wisdom of Creator God who gave us our genders? (Gen. 1:26-28 / Mark 10:6). Gender assignment is determined by

God in the womb not determined by feelings or human reasoning (Ps. 139:13-16).

THE CURE

What is the cure for the unbelieving, carnal mind? Let's look in Matthew 17 at the same account of the father with the demoniac son we read earlier from Mark. Matthew brings out something different than Mark. In this account the disciples come to Jesus privately and ask why they couldn't cast the demon out. Obviously, they had done this before, but for some reason it didn't work this time, and they wanted to know the reason. In Mark, Jesus said that this kind only comes out by prayer and fasting (Mk. 9:29). Many people think in error that Jesus was referring to the demon, but He clears that up here in Matthew 17:19-21— *"Then the disciples came to Jesus privately and said, 'Why could we not cast it out?' So Jesus said to them, 'Because of your **unbelief** for assuredly, I say to you, if you have faith as a mustard seed, you will say to this mountain, 'Move from here to there,' and it will move; and nothing will be impossible for you. However, this kind does not go out except by prayer and fasting.'"* Jesus gives them the answer here; it was because of their unbelief. Then He goes on to give them the cure—prayer and fasting. Demons do not come out by prayer and fasting. That idea is found nowhere in Scripture; however, we do need to pray and fast to discipline our senses and carnal, unrenewed minds. Prayer and fasting aren't for the purpose of getting God to move, but they move us to where God is working and flowing.

Prayer and fasting casts out this kind of unbelief, leaving a pure faith which can believe only and cast out any demon. When that boy fell on the ground foaming at the mouth the disciples got shook. They doubted their authority and power over demons because of this dramatic demonic manifestation. They believed what they saw more than what Jesus told them. This moment revealed the carnal mindedness of the disciples, and Jesus told them that prayer and fasting would deal with that carnality. When the man brought the boy to Jesus, the demon tried the same trick on Jesus; however, He was unmoved and unimpressed. Jesus was not moved by what He saw but He believed only.

The apostle Paul addressed this concerning himself in 1 Corinthians 9:27— *"But I discipline my* **body** *and bring it into subjection, lest, when I have preached to others, I myself should become disqualified."* If you look at the context of this scripture you see that he is comparing this to an athlete who has to train the body to win the prize. Paul is saying that he doesn't let his senses dominate him. He isn't denying his five physical senses of seeing, hearing, smelling, tasting, and feeling; he just doesn't let them control him. This is what prayer and fasting accomplish.

Paul also refers to this in Romans 12:1— *"I beseech you therefore brethren, by the mercies of God that you present your bodies a* **living sacrifice**, *holy, acceptable to God, which is your reasonable service."* This is not suggesting that we kill our bodies but rather recognize that they are in a fallen condition and must be submitted to God. In other words, being in this world but not of it (Jn. 17:16). This is how we can combat the unbelief that is driven by our physical senses.

Prayer and Fasting

Prayer and fasting are powerful tools for the believer who wants to eradicate unbelief and carnal thinking. But, most Christians either do not fast or have a misconstrued idea about fasting. Many Christians who do fast have an old covenant mindset about it, thinking they need to fast to get God to move, change His mind, or do something they want Him to do. They have no idea the purpose of fasting under the new covenant, so their misguided attempts are more like a hunger strike than a spiritual discipline. God is not motivated by your hunger strike. If He hasn't already moved in grace, then you are not going to be able to move Him in works of faith. Our faith moves mountains, Satan, circumstances, and our own hearts; but faith does not move God. Faith appropriates and receives what God has already provided in grace.

Jesus taught that our motives are extremely important in fasting (Matt. 6:16-18). What is the purpose? A lot of people fast to get God to speak thinking they can storm the altar, grab hold of the horns and hold on until God speaks. In reality, God is speaking all the time. We are often unable to hear because of carnality and being focused on worldly things. Too many times we are caught up in the affairs of this life and unable to let our minds get quiet enough to hear that still, small voice of Holy Spirit on the inside of us.

While fasting doesn't move God, it does move us closer to where God is. It won't get God to speak, but it can shut down our carnal senses and the voices of the world. 1 Corinthians 14:10 tells us— *"There are, it may be, so many kinds of languages in the world, and none of them is without significance."* We are surrounded by voices clamoring for our attention making it difficult to hear what God is saying especially when our five physical senses are dominating us. So, in its simplest form, fasting brings our senses and carnal, unrenewed minds under subjection to God's Word and His will.

Thinking of a radio signal helps illustrate this point. There are signals in the air all around us, but we need a transmitter to hear them. There is music playing, but you need a transmitter in order to tune in to the station and electromagnetic waves to hear the music clearly. The Holy Spirit is speaking, but we have to get still and tune in to the voice of the Lord. The only way to do that is to tune out the voices of the world and the voice of our carnal mind. Sometimes it is hard to hear God clearly because of all the clamor, especially the voices of our past, parents, spouse, employer, etc. When we dwell on the wrong voices, we let how we feel become more important than what the Bible says. That is why our cry needs to be, "I believe, help my unbelief!" The disciples could have said, "Lord we believe, help our unbelief." Jesus would have then said, "This kind of unbelief comes out or is cured by fasting and praying."

Fasting and prayer shut down our carnal, unrenewed minds and bring our five physical senses into subjection to God's authority. This is what Jesus was explaining when He answered the disciple's question. He told them that they had let what they saw and felt dominate them rather than faith in God. He identified that they were operating in unbelief. The disciples and the boy's father were influenced more by sight and feelings than God's Word and will. It was their unbelief that needed to be dealt with by fasting and prayer. These disciplines cast out unbelief so the devil or demon can be cast out in faith. Faith casts out all demons whereas prayer and fasting cast out this kind of unbelief.

As believers, we are saved from the wrath to come. God's righteous judgment will come and there will be a new heaven and a new earth where nothing but righteousness will remain (Rom. 5:8-10 / 1 Thess. 1:10). There we will rule and reign with the Lord forever with our resurrected new bodies. However, until then, we have this natural man we must contend with having a choice every day: are we going to walk after the flesh or after the Spirit? The key is to have our minds set on the things of God rather than this world. Prayer and fasting help us be formed into the image of Jesus and lose our appetites for worldliness. These disciplines starve out our unbelief and make us vessels that can more clearly tune into what the Spirit is doing and saying. We are in this world, but we do not have to be of it and operate according to its dictates.

SYMPTOMS OF UNBELIEF

If any of you lacks wisdom, let him ask of God, who gives to all liberally and without reproach, and it will be given to him. But let him ask in faith, with no doubting, for he who doubts is like a wave of the sea driven and tossed by wind. For let not that man suppose that he will **receive anything** *from the Lord; he is a double-minded man, unstable in all his ways.*

James 1:5-8

Here, James talks about a couple of symptoms of unbelief—doubting and wavering. God is not withholding from us, but we must ask in faith without doubting or wavering. Unbelief can cause double-mindedness and instability making it impossible to receive from the Lord. We can't blame God thinking He is holding out on us. He's giving, we just can't receive because of unbelief.

Matthew 14:28-31 tells the story of Peter walking on water. What a miracle! This man jumped out of a boat and walked on the sea, following one word from Jesus, "come." Then look what happens when

Peter gets his eyes off Jesus and looks at the wind and waves; it says in verse 30— *"But when he saw that the wind was boisterous, he was afraid; and beginning to sink he cried out, saying, 'Lord save me!'"* Over the years I have asked myself what does wind and waves have to do with water-walking? Could I walk on calm water? No, it doesn't work. Try it. Fill up your bathtub and try to walk on the water. You'll see that even calm water doesn't make for easy water-walking. So, Peter walking on the sea towards Jesus is truly a miracle and an act of faith. The wind had nothing to do with this miracle. Once Peter abandoned his eyes from Jesus and focused on the circumstances around him, he **began** to sink. He didn't just suddenly go from water-walking to sinking, he started to sink and cried out to the Lord. Jesus grabbed Peter by the hand and led him back to the boat where He chided him for doubting. Faith got Peter on the water, but doubt came in and caused him to lose focus and sink.

Peter's example should motivate us to discern unbelief in our own lives, which can be tricky because it tends to disguise itself. But unbelief can be discerned when we know its symptoms. A good example of this is murmuring and complaining. Murmuring and complaining is the voice of unbelief, not faith. The voice of faith is thanksgiving. Fear, worry, and anxiety are also symptoms of unbelief. When fear has our attention, it gets worse; it grows bigger and bigger. We don't have to ignore it or deny fear, we just need to recognize it as the feeling of unbelief and deal with it. Just like there is a feeling of unbelief, there is a feeling of belief; it is called joy and peace. This feeling comes when you focus on the Word of God and His promises (Is. 26:3).

Unbelief also can lead us to feel disqualified. No matter what God has called us to do we can be tempted to feel unworthy of his call. When we fall into this pattern of thinking, it is evidence that unbelief is at work in how we see ourselves. Here is the good news—God doesn't call qualified servants to preach, lead, or minister, but instead, He qualifies those called by His grace:

But God has chosen the foolish things of the world to put to shame the wise, and God has chosen the weak things of the world to put to shame the things which are mighty; and the base things of the world and the things which are despised God has chosen, and the things which are not, to bring to nothing the things that are, that no flesh should glory in His presence.

1 Corinthians 1:27-29

God chose us and called us from before creation (Eph. 1:4). Before we ever did anything right or wrong, God called us. He doesn't call the qualified, He qualifies the called! Unbelief says we are not qualified, but faith says we are qualified by God's grace. Praise the Lord! Our worthiness isn't dependent on our works, but on Christ and His Spirit; we just need to walk after the Spirit and not our flesh. The sooner we learn to discern the voices of unbelief through its various symptoms, the sooner we will see God's Kingdom advance in a more powerful way than we ever imagined.

Conclusion

All of us face situations where we believe but need help with our unbelief. My prayer is that we all transition to where we "believe only." May we put into practice the cures for unbelief and uncover the places where unbelief tries to hide in our hearts. Let God be true and every man, feeling, or circumstance contrary to truth, be a liar. Thanks be unto God who gives us the victory over unbelief in Christ Jesus our Lord (2 Cor. 2:14).

Salvation Prayer

If your heart desires connection with your Heavenly Father and to live in the blessing of His family, there is hope in Christ Jesus. If you have not made Jesus Lord of your life but would like to do so, you can simply pray this:

"Father, I come to you today; I confess I'm not right, but I want to be right and make things right. I cannot do enough or quit enough to save myself, I need help. I believe Jesus is that help. I believe He came to this earth, lived a perfect life, and died on the cross for me. He bore my sins and the punishment for all my sins. He died, was buried, and rose again on the third day. I now confess Him as Lord, King, and Savior. Thank you for forgiving me and cleansing me of all my sin and changing me in my heart. Help me now to serve you all the days of my life, with all my heart. Amen!"

If you prayed this prayer and received Jesus in your heart today, let us know and we will send you a free book! Contact us at 580-634-5665 or dsm@pastorduane.com

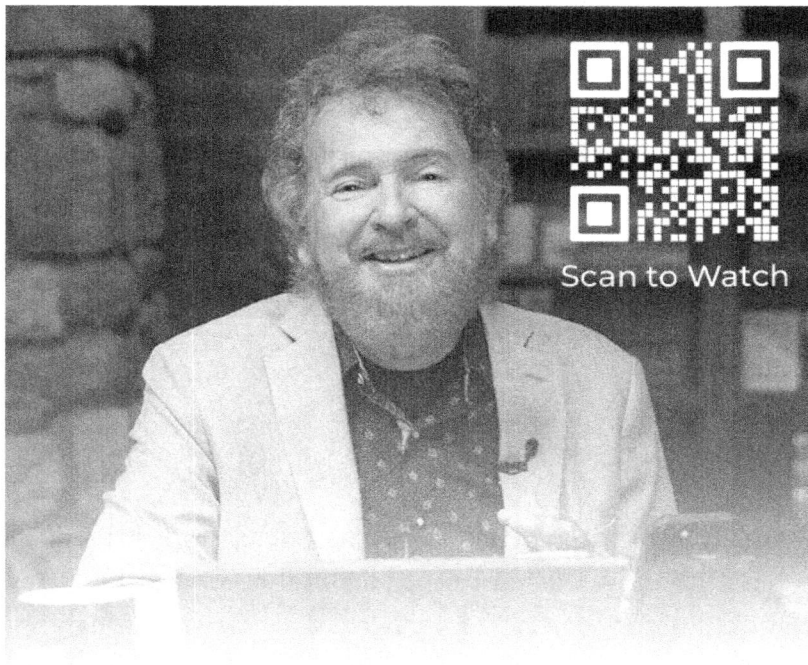

Scan to Watch

GRACE & TRUTH

Join Duane as he boldly teaches Biblical wisdom mixed with his unique sense of humor, offering hope & revelation for today's world.

About The Author

Duane Sheriff has been in ministry for over four decades. He is an author, international apostolic teacher, conference speaker and founder of Victory Life Church. He is known for his humor and ability to present the Gospel with clarity and simplicity. He is passionate about helping people discover their identity and grow in Christ through his unique biblical insights.

His first book, *Identity Theft*, was released in 2017. Since then, he has authored several more books including: *Divine Guidance, Rhythms of Grace, Erasing Offense, and Counterculture*. He also serves as an adjunct instructor at Charis Bible School, and hosts "Grace & Truth," a daily television broadcast. Duane and his wife, Sue, were married in 1980 and have four children, who have blessed them with numerous grandchildren.

For additional study resources or free teachings visit our website at **www.pastorduane.com**

CONTACT INFORMATION

Duane Sheriff Ministries

PO Box 427, Durant, OK

dsm@pastorduane.com

Helpline (Mon. – Fri. 8am-5pm CT)

580-404-0376

www.pastorduane.com

Printed in Great Britain
by Amazon

54906376R00036